IT'S TIME TO EAT BANANA WHEAT BREAD

It's Time to Eat BANANA WHEAT BREAD

Walter the Educator

Silent King Books
A WhichHead Entertainment Imprint

Copyright © 2025 by Walter the Educator

All rights reserved. No part of this book may be reproduced in any manner whatsoever without written per- mission except in the case of brief quotations embodied in critical articles and reviews.

First Printing, 2024

Disclaimer

This book is a literary work; the story is not about specific persons, locations, situations, and/or circumstances unless mentioned in a historical context. Any resemblance to real persons, locations, situations, and/or circumstances is coincidental. This book is for entertainment and informational purposes only. The author and publisher offer this information without warranties expressed or implied. No matter the grounds, neither the author nor the publisher will be accountable for any losses, injuries, or other damages caused by the reader's use of this book. The use of this book acknowledges an understanding and acceptance of this disclaimer.

It's Time to Eat BANANA WHEAT BREAD is a collectible early learning book by Walter the Educator suitable for all ages belonging to Walter the Educator's Time to Eat Book Series. Collect more books at WaltertheEducator.com

USE THE EXTRA SPACE TO TAKE NOTES AND DOCUMENT YOUR MEMORIES

BANANA WHEAT BREAD

The smell is sweet, the time is near,

It's Time to Eat
Banana Wheat Bread

Banana wheat bread, let's all cheer!

Golden brown and warm inside,

A yummy treat we won't let slide!

The oven beeps, it's time to see,

A loaf so soft and tasty, whee!

Slice it up and take a bite,

Oh, this snack is pure delight!

Bananas ripe and oh so sweet,

Mixed with wheat to make a treat.

Soft and fluffy, rich and grand,

Baked with love and made by hand.

Spread some butter, watch it melt,

The warmest joy I've ever felt!

Maybe honey, maybe jam,

Any topping, yes, I am!

It's Time to Eat Banana Wheat Bread

Morning, noon, or late at night,

Banana bread feels just right.

A glass of milk, a sip of tea,

A perfect snack for you and me!

One more bite, okay, just two,

It's so good, I can't be through!

Soft and chewy, yum, yum, yum,

I tap my plate and rub my tum!

Mom and Dad, come have some, too!

There's enough for all of you!

Friends can join, just grab a seat,

Banana bread is fun to eat!

Look inside, surprise, oh my!

Some walnuts make it extra fly!

Or maybe chocolate chips so sweet,

It's Time to Eat
Banana
Wheat
Bread

Each new slice is such a treat!

Let's bake more, don't wait too long,

Mix and mash and sing a song!

Flour, eggs, and fruit so fine,

Stir it up, it's baking time!

The timer dings, it's time again,

Banana bread, our snack-time friend!

Let's all share, let's all smile,

It's Time to Eat
Banana Wheat Bread

Banana wheat bread's best by miles!

ABOUT THE CREATOR

Walter the Educator is one of the pseudonyms for Walter Anderson. Formally educated in Chemistry, Business, and Education, he is an educator, an author, a diverse entrepreneur, and he is the son of a disabled war veteran. "Walter the Educator" shares his time between educating and creating. He holds interests and owns several creative projects that entertain, enlighten, enhance, and educate, hoping to inspire and motivate you. Follow, find new works, and stay up to date with Walter the Educator™

at WaltertheEducator.com

www.ingramcontent.com/pod-product-compliance
Lightning Source LLC
La Vergne TN
LVHW010622070526
838199LV00063BA/5240